THE PUEBLOS

A TRUE BOOK

by

Alice K. Flanagan

Children's Press®
A Division of Grolier Publishing
New York London Hong Kong Sydney
Danbury, Connecticut

Pueblo ruins

Reading Consultant
Linda Cornwell
Learning Resource Consultant
Indiana Department
of Education

Visit Children's Press on the Internet at:
http://publishing.grolier.com

Library of Congress Cataloging-in-Publication Data

Flanagan, Alice K.
  The Pueblos / by Alice K. Flanagan.
    p.   cm. — (A True book)
  Includes index.
  Summary: Examines the culture, history, and society of the Pueblos.
  ISBN 0–516–20626–5 (lib. bdg.)   0-516-26383-8 (pbk.)
  1. Pueblo Indians—History—Juvenile literature. 2. Pueblo Indians—
Social life and customs—Juvenile literature. [1. Pueblo Indians.
  2. Indians of North America—Southwest, New.] I. Title. II. Series.
E99.P9F57 1998
973'04974—dc21   97–12683
                                                       CIP
                                                        AC

Contents

People of the Rio Grande   5

Walking with the Ancient Ones   12

Creating Beauty   16

Pueblo Homes   22

Agriculture and Family Life   27

Dancing with the Spirits   32

Surviving Change   39

To Find Out More   44

Important Words   46

Index   47

Meet the Author   48

The Rio Grande flows from the Rocky Mountains to the Gulf of Mexico.

People of the Rio Grande

In the southwestern United States is a river called the Rio Grande. Here, along its banks, you can find one of the oldest civilizations in North America. The people who built the civilization are ancestors of the Pueblos (PWEB-los). They and their

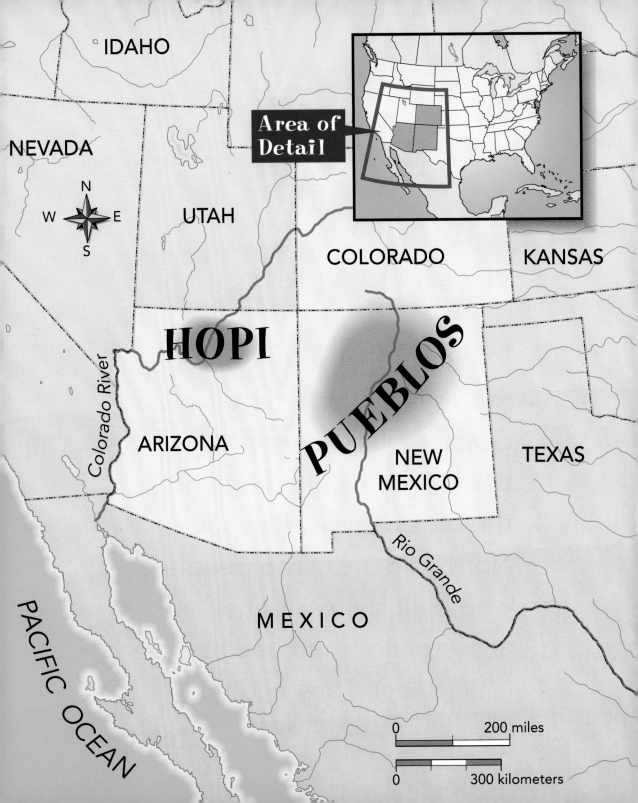

IDAHO

NEVADA

W N E S

UTAH

Area of
Detail

COLORADO

KANSAS

HOPI

PUEBLOS

Colorado River

ARIZONA

NEW
MEXICO

TEXAS

MEXICO

Rio Grande

PACIFIC OCEAN

0   200 miles

0   300 kilometers

descendants—today's Pueblo Americans—have been farming the land for thousands of years.

Pueblo means "village" in Spanish. In the 1500s, Spanish explorers gave this name to the people they found living in well-organized communities of apartment-like houses.

Spanish explorers who saw these buildings were reminded of their own villages in Spain. So they decided to call them *pueblos.*

Pueblos also refers to the people who live in the villages.

Today, the word *pueblo* means both the type of homes these people built (pueblos), and the people who built them (the Pueblos).

The Pueblos are descendants of two ancient peoples called the Mogollon (mo-go-YONE) and Anasazi (ana-SA-zee).

Today, there are nineteen Pueblo groups. They all share their ancestors' religious beliefs and lifestyles, but each group has its own name and customs that make it unique.

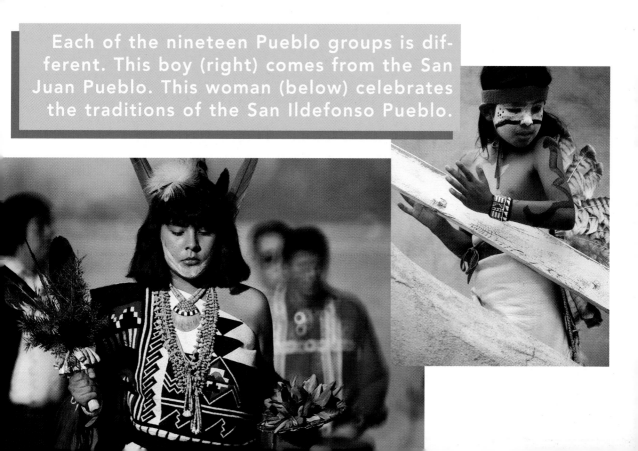

Each of the nineteen Pueblo groups is different. This boy (right) comes from the San Juan Pueblo. This woman (below) celebrates the traditions of the San Ildefonso Pueblo.

The present-day Pueblos still live in the villages that the Spaniards invaded during the sixteenth century and claimed for the king of Spain. Sixteen of these villages rise from the land that winds along a 130-mile (210-kilometer) stretch of the Rio Grande to the Gulf of Mexico. Another three villages lie west of the great river. The Hopi Indians in Arizona are also part of the Pueblo family.

The Pueblo Villages

The Taos Pueblo village

NEW MEXICO

Area of Detail

Taos
Picuris
Santa Clara
San Juan
San Ildefonso
Pojoaque
Nambe
Cochiti
Tesuque
Jemez
Santo Domingo
Zia
Santa Ana
San Felipe
Rio Grande
Zuni
Laguna
Sandia
Acoma
Isleta

0   20 miles
0   30 kilometers

Nineteen Pueblo villages are currently located in the southwestern United States. A different Pueblo group lives in each village. Here's how you say their names:

Taos (TAH-os)
Picuris (pick-oo-RIS)
Nambe (nam-BAY)
Pojoaque (po-HUA-kay)
San Ildefonso (san eel-dee-FON-zo)
Tesuque (tay-SOO-kay)
San Juan (san WHAN)
Santa Clara (SAN-ta CLA-ra)
Zuni (zoo-NEE)
Acoma (AH-coma)

Jemez (HAY-mes)
Cochiti (COACH-ee-tee)
Sandia (san-DEE-ah)
San Felipe (san Fe-LEEP-ay)
Santa Ana (SAN-ta A-na)
Santo Domingo (SAN-to doh-MIN-goh)
Zia (ZEE-ah)
Isleta (ees-LET-ah)
Laguna (la-GOON-ah)

Walking with the Ancient Ones

Among the many things Pueblos share are stories of their ancestors and how their life began. In the beginning, they say, their ancestors came from the north, where they had emerged from the under-world through a lake. Slowly,

The ruins of communities built by Pueblo ancestors are now protected as national parks.

over thousands of years, the people traveled south and settled in the present-day states of Nevada, Utah, Colorado, Arizona, New Mexico, Texas, and northeastern Mexico. They thrived in the mostly dry land because they knew how to grow and harvest crops. Today, remains of these early communities are protected as national parks and monuments.

The Mogollon, or "Mountain People," settled in southwestern New Mexico. Some made their homes in cliffs. Others lived in pit houses dug partly underground.

Northeast of the Mogollons, where the borders of the present states of New Mexico, Arizona, Colorado, and Utah

meet, the Anasazi, or "Ancient Ones," lived. They built great cities connected by a network of roads. Between A.D. 700 and 1300, Chaco Canyon in central New Mexico was a great center of trade and religious activity.

Creating Beauty

Skilled basketmakers, the Anasazi wove fine sandals and containers from different plant fibers. Not only were they masters at weaving, they were also known for their painted pottery, brightly colored cotton clothing, and beautiful turquoise jewelry.

An Anasazi jar

After the Anasazi moved to
the Rio Grande valley, they
mined turquoise. This stone
was considered a symbol of
wealth and an important item
of trade. Today, blue-and-

This bear figurine is decorated with a turquoise necklace.

green turquoise is a very popular stone used in making jewelry, especially among the Zuni.

Pueblo artists have been making pottery since prehistoric times. They are known the world over for their unique patterns and shapes. They gather the clay from local sites and mold it into containers or fig- urines, which they paint and then heat over fire. Julian and Maria Martinez from San Ildefonso Pueblo have created a black-on-black pottery design that is unique.

A Pueblo artist molds the clay into a jar and then decorates it with painted patterns.

Cochiti and Tesuque potters are famous for their delightful figurines. Miniature figures from Tesuque represent the daily activities of Pueblo life. Figurines called "storytellers" were created in 1964 by Helen Cordero, a Cochiti potter. She made a clay figure to represent her grandfather telling stories to his grandchildren who were seated on his lap. She kept his eyes closed to show him

thinking as he sang. Today, there are many versions of this first storyteller. Each figure carries a batch of playful children or animals.

Pueblo Homes

In about A.D. 1300, the
Anasazi abandoned their
cities and moved to sites
along the Rio Grande and the
Little Colorado River. In the
new environment, they found
a new way to build houses.
Using clay, which was abun-
dant in the area, they made

When these slabs of mud dry, they will be used as adobe bricks.

structures of stone and mud (adobe) or of sun-dried adobe bricks and straw. The first houses were single-family homes. But when raids upon villages became more frequent, people built apartment-like dwellings to protect themselves against attackers.

The walls of these high-rise buildings had few doors or windows on the ground level. People entered through holes in the roofs. The flat roofs of the lower level became the floor and front yard of the upper level. All the levels were connected by ladders, which were carefully guarded

Many modern Pueblos still use ladders to enter their homes.

and pulled up after everyone was inside.

Although some people still live in these dwellings, many of these structures are now used as centers of worship or for social activities. Some are being replaced by new single-

Brick adobe has been the main building material in the Southwest for hundreds of years.

family homes. Brick adobe is still the Pueblos' material of choice when building homes because it is so well-suited to New Mexico's climate.

Agriculture and Family Life

In the past, Pueblos support-
ed their large villages by
farming. Each family had its
own land for gardening, but
every member of the commu-
nity helped everyone else.
Families lived together in
groups called clans. The clans

had names such as Eagle, Bear, and Sun. Usually, women were the head of the household. They owned the property and passed on their names to their children.

Because water was scarce, people built irrigation ditches

Water is a precious resource for the Pueblos.

to gather rainwater and control the precious water supply. Carefully, they watered their crops of beans, sunflowers, squash, pumpkins, tobacco, cotton, and corn of many colors. Corn was the main crop.

A Pueblo woman stands in front of a domed bread oven.

From it they made cornmeal mush, hominy, and a mixture of beans and corn called succotash. In outdoor ovens, they made many different kinds of breads and cakes. Tortillas and a very thin bread called piki are still popular today.

To add to their diet, Pueblos hunted small game such as deer, antelope, and rabbits. They also gathered fruits and nuts. They kept tame dogs and turkeys as pets, often using turkey feathers for decorations.

Dancing with the Spirits

Pueblos believe that everything in life has a soul or spirit that gives it special power to be what it is. Earth is "Mother." She nurtures the seeds planted in her and allows them to become food for the people. Sky is "Father." Under his care, the sun, moon, rain, wind, and clouds help seeds to grow.

Each season, Pueblos hold special ceremonies in which they dance with the spirits. Some of the ceremonies are performed secretly in under-ground chambers called kivas.

Others are conducted above ground in the open. The people who have a special part in the ceremonies are called kachinas. They paint their bodies, wear masks carved to honor the spirits, and mimic them through dance and song. When kachinas dance, they and their ancestors become one.

In earlier times, people held ceremonies for rain. In the winter, they asked the spirits for snow. In the fall, they thanked

Santa Clara Pueblos perform a corn dance.

the ancestors for the good harvest and for successful hunts.

Prayers had to be said in just
the right way before the spirits
would answer them. Many of
these prayer dances have
become the Pueblo ceremonial
dances of today. At different

Pueblo eagle
dancers (above) and
deer dancers (left)

times of the year, Pueblos participate in these ceremonies
that may include kachinas,
corn maidens, clowns (called
mud-heads), or dancers that

represent animals such as but-
terflies, eagles, buffalo, or
deer. Today, carved dolls of
these dancers are collected
around the world.

Pueblos also hold festivals
to honor Roman Catholic
feast-day traditions and
patron saints. Although these
celebrations were introduced
by the Spaniards who occu-
pied the Pueblo country in the
sixteenth century, they are
now part of Pueblo tradition.

The Kiva

The kiva is a special chamber built underground. There is only one entrance, through the roof. Inside, sacred ceremonies take place in which kachina dancers and spirits become one. On the walls, paintings display important Pueblo symbols or ceremonies. There are several kivas in each Pueblo village.

The only way into or out of the kiva is by climbing a ladder. Murals are painted on the walls.

Surviving Change

After the Pueblos settled in their present homeland, they were ruled by three powerful countries—first Spain, then Mexico, and finally the United States. Each took control of their land and forced them to follow new religious beliefs and a way of life foreign to them.

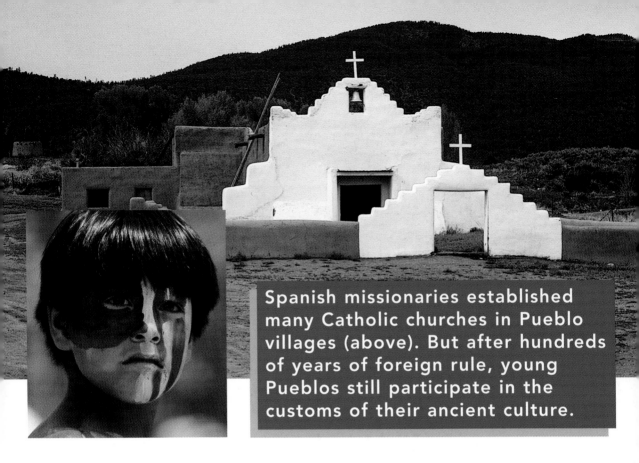

Spanish missionaries established many Catholic churches in Pueblo villages (above). But after hundreds of years of foreign rule, young Pueblos still participate in the customs of their ancient culture.

In 1539, Spanish explorers came to the American Southwest in search of treasures. From 1540 to 1680, soldiers and Catholic missionaries followed. Without regard for

Pueblo culture, they took over villages, renamed them, and built churches to replace the native religion. Those who did not follow their rules were killed or enslaved.

The Pueblos rebelled against Spanish rule in 1680 and drove the Spaniards from their land. But Spanish troops returned in 1692 and regained control. The Pueblos remained under Spanish rule until 1821, when Mexico gained its independence from Spain. Mexico ruled until 1848, when the United States took the land after a war with Mexico. In 1924, Pueblos were made citizens of the United States.

Pueblos cherish their native culture and their sacred connection to the spirit world. But they are also Americans with a Spanish past. These traditions make them who they are.

Through drama, song, and dance, Pueblos continue to tell the story of their people to each new generation and

to bring to earth the power of the Holy Ones. They work together through the All-Indian Pueblo Council to protect their sacred lands and to make life better for all the people in the world.

To Find Out More

Here are some additional resources to help you learn more about the Pueblos:

Books

Bartok, Mira, and Christine Ronan. **Pueblo Indians of the Southwest.** Good Year Books, 1995.

Flanagan, Alice K. **The Zunis.** Children's Press, 1998.

Fradin, Dennis. **Sea to Shining Sea: New Mexico.** Children's Press, 1994.

Hallet, Bill and Jill Hallet. **Pueblo Indians of New Mexico: Activities and Adventures for Children.** Look & See, 1991.

Hoyt-Goldsmith, Diane. **Pueblo Storyteller.** Holiday, 1994.

Miller, Jay. **American Indian Festivals.** Children's Press, 1996.

Powell, Suzanne. **The Pueblos.** Franklin Watts, 1993.

Organizations and Online Sites

Anasazi Archaeology
http://www.swcolo.org/ Tourism/ArchaeologyHome .html

An exciting site with several pages of Anasazi ruins.

Chetro Ketl Great Kiva
http://www.sscf.ucsb.edu/ anth/projects/great.kiva/ index.html

An incredible site that allows the viewer to take a virtual reality tour of a kiva as it probably appeared hundreds of years ago. The site includes a recording of the music and chants that may have been performed.

The Heard Museum: Native Cultures and Art
http://hanksville.phast. umass.edu/defs/ independent/Heard/

Museum site that exhibits American Indian Art in the Southwest.

Indian Pueblo Cultural Center
http://www.viva.com/nm/ PCCmirror/PCC.html#toc

This site provides links to the nineteen individual Pueblo groups.

Murals of the Indian Pueblo Cultural Center
http://hanksville.phast.umass. edu/defs/independent/PCC/ murals.html

A site that provides illustrations of several colorful Pueblo murals.

Native American Navigator
http://www.ilt.columbia. edu/k12/naha/nanav.html

A general site with hundreds of links to topics on Native Americans.

Pueblo Cultural Center
2401 12th Street NW
(1 block North of I-40)
Albuquerque, New Mexico
87192

Cultural center that presents and preserves the heritage of the nineteen Pueblo groups.

New Mexico's Cultural Treasures
http://www.nmculture.org/

A central index that lists the museums, monuments, and natural wonders of New Mexico.

Important Words

adobe muddy mixture that is dried into bricks

ancestors people who came before

clan collection of families living together

irrigation ditch dug-out trench that allows water to reach crops

kachina special dancer who imitates the spirits

kiva underground chamber where special ceremonies take place

piki thin bread

potter person who works with clay to make pots or bowls

succotash mixture of beans and corn

Index

(**Boldface** page numbers
indicate illustrations.)

adobe, **23,** 23–24, 26, **26**
All-Indian Pueblo
   Council, 43
Anasazi, 8, 15, 16, 22
Ancient Ones, 15
Arizona, 10, 13, 14
Chaco Canyon, 15
clans, 27–28
Cochiti, 20
Colorado, 13, 14
cooking, 30–31, **30**
Cordero, Helen, 20
corn, **29**
dance, 33–37, **35, 36,**
   42, **43**
Hopi, 10
kachina, 34
kiva, 33, **38**
Little Colorado River, 22
Mexico, 13, 39, 41–42
Mogollon, 8, 14

New Mexico, 13, 14, 15,
   26
Nevada, 13
pottery, 16, **17,** 18–19,
   18, 19, 20–21, **21**
pueblo communities,
   7–8, **7, 11,** 13–14, **13**
Rio Grande, **4,** 5, 10, 22
Roman Catholicism, 37,
   40
San Ildefonso Pueblo, **9**
San Juan Pueblo, **9**
Southwestern United
   States, 5, 11, 40
Spain, 7, 39
Spaniards, 7, 10, 37, 40,
   41
spirits, 32–38
Tesuque, 20
Texas, 13
Turquoise, 16–18, **18**
United States, 39, 42
Utah, 13, 14
water, **28,** 28–29

Meet the Author

Alice Flanagan thinks of the world as an open book filled with living stories. As an author, she thinks of herself as an observer—one who watches the stories as they unfold, then carefully writes them down.

Once a teacher, Ms. Flanagan taught Native American children in South Dakota and New Mexico. She feels blessed by the wonderful gifts they shared. Now, through her writing, she tries to pass these gifts on to others. In the True Book: Native Americans series, Ms. Flanagan is the author of the following titles. *The Eskimo, The Chippewa, The Navajo, The Nez Perce, The Pueblos, The Shawnee, The Sioux, The Tlingit, The Utes, The Wampanoags,* and *The Zunis.* Ms. Flanagan lives with her husband in Chicago, Illinois.